# Guitar Notation Legend

**THE MUSICAL STAFF** shows pitches and rhythms and is divided by bar lines into measures. Pitches are named after the first seven letters of the alphabet.

**TABLATURE** graphically represents the guitar fingerboard. Each horizontal line represents a string, and each number represents a fret.

4th string, 2nd fret    1st & 2nd strings open, played together    open D

**HALF-STEP BEND:** Strike the note and bend up 1/2 step.

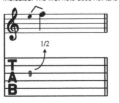

**WHOLE-STEP BEND:** Strike the note and bend up one step.

**GRACE NOTE BEND:** Strike the note a indicated. The first note does not take up

**BEND AND RELEASE:** Strike the note and bend up as indicated, then release back to the original note. Only the first note is struck.

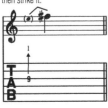

**PRE-BEND:** Bend the note as indicated, then strike it.

**VIBRATO:** The string is vibrated by rapidly bending and releasing the note with the fretting hand.

**PALM MUTING:** The note is partially muted by the pick hand lightly touching the string(s) just before the bridge.

**HAMMER-ON:** Strike the first (lower) note with one finger, then sound the higher note (on the same string) with another finger by fretting it without picking.

**PULL-OFF:** Place both fingers on the notes to be sounded. Strike the first note and without picking, pull the finger off to sound the second (lower) note.

**LEGATO SLIDE:** Strike the first note and then slide the same fret-hand finger up or down to the second note. The second note is not struck.

**SHIFT SLIDE:** Same as legato slide, except the second note is struck.

**TRILL:** Very rapidly alternate between the notes indicated by continuously hammering on and pulling off.

**TAPPING:** Hammer ("tap") the fret indicated with the pick-hand index or middle finger and pull off to the note fretted by the fret hand.

**NATURAL HARMONIC:** Strike the note while the fret-hand lightly touches the string directly over the fret indicated.

**PINCH HARMONIC:** The note is fretted normally and a harmonic is produced by adding the edge of the thumb or the tip of the index finger of the pick hand to the normal pick attack.

**TREMOLO PICKING:** The note is picked as rapidly and continuously as possible.

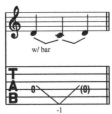

**VIBRATO BAR DIVE AND RETURN:** The pitch of the note or chord is dropped a specified number of steps (in rhythm) then returned to the original pitch.

**VIBRATO BAR SCOOP:** Depress the bar just before striking the note, then quickly release the bar.

**VIBRATO BAR DIP:** Strike the note and then immediately drop a specified number of steps, then release back to the original pitch.

# Additional Musical Definitions

 *(accent)* • Accentuate note (play it louder)

**Fill** • Label used to identify a brief melodic figure which is to be inserted into the arrangement.

 *(staccato)* • Play the note short

**N.C.** • No Chord

***D.S. al Coda*** • Go back to the sign (𝄋), then play until the measure marked ***"To Coda"***, then skip to the section labelled ***"Coda."***

• Repeat measures between signs.

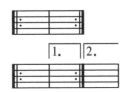

***D.C. al Fine*** • Go back to the beginning of the song and play until the measure marked ***"Fine"*** (end).

• When a repeated section has different endings, play the first ending only the first time and the second ending only the second time.

5

# Beverly Hills

## Words and Music by Rivers Cuomo

Tune down 1/2 step:
(low to high) Eb-Ab-Db-Gb-Bb-Eb

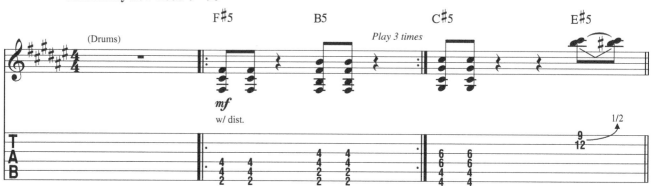

**Verse**

____ I'm just a no-class beat-down fool and I will al-ways be that

way. I might as well ___ en-joy my life and watch the stars play.

*D.S. al Coda*

**Coda**

**Outro-Chorus**

Bev - er - ly Hills, _____

w/ dist.

hold bend

9

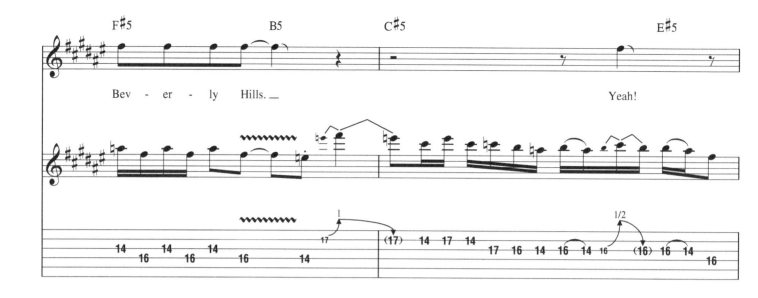

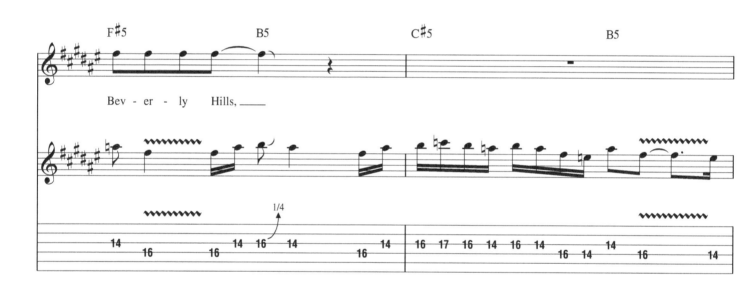

*Additional Lyrics*

2. Look at all those movie stars, they're all so beautiful and clean.
  When the housemaids scrub the floors they get the spaces in between.
  I wanna live a life like that, I wanna be just like a king.
  Take my picture by the pool 'cause I'm the next big thing in...

# Hash Pipe

**Words and Music by Rivers Cuomo**

**Outro**

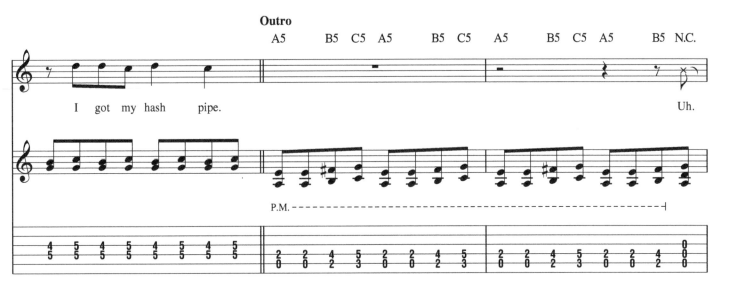

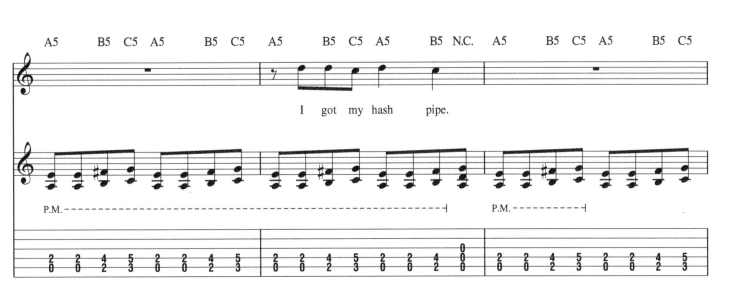

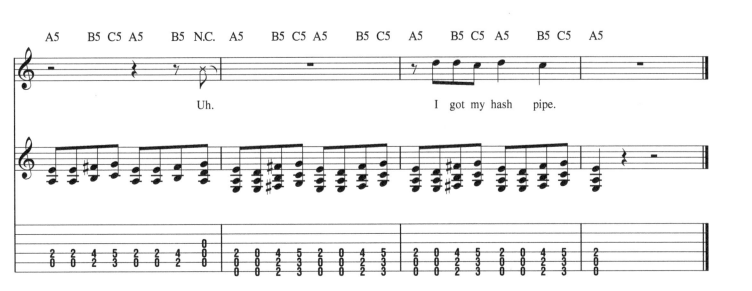

*Additional Lyrics*

2. I can't help my boogies, they get out of control.
I know that you don't care but I want you to know.
The knee stocking flavor is a favorite treat
Of men that don't bother with the taste of a teat.

# Buddy Holly

**Words and Music by Rivers Cuomo**

*Bass plays notes to right of slash.

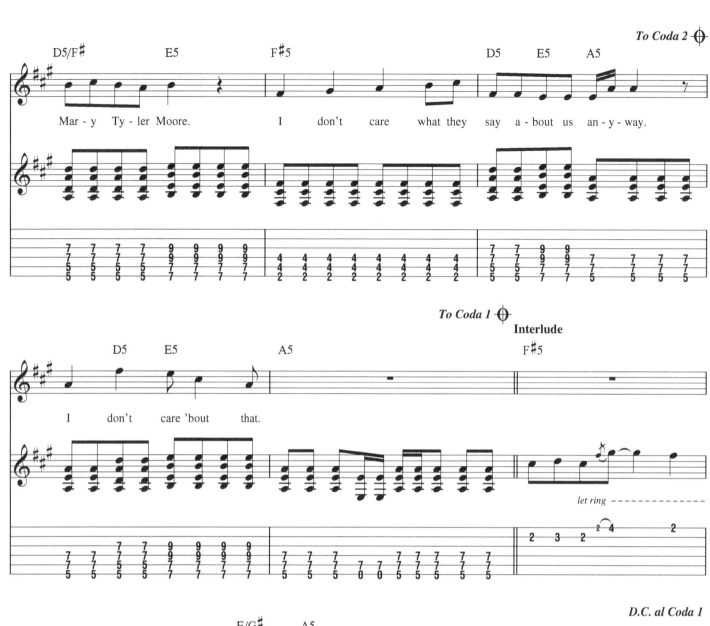

*To Coda 1*

**Interlude**

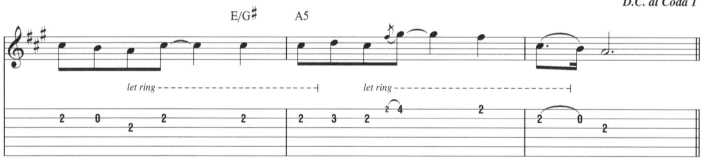

*D.C. al Coda 1*

**Coda 1**

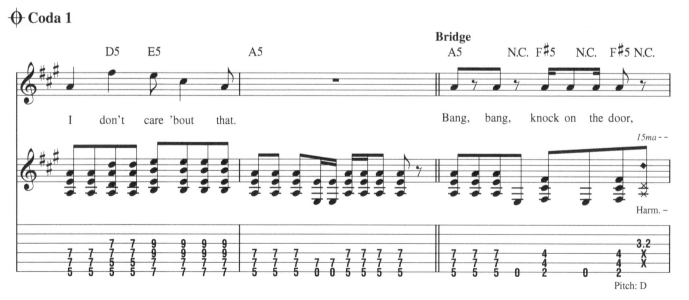

'noth-er big bang, you're down _ on the floor. Oh no, what do I do? _

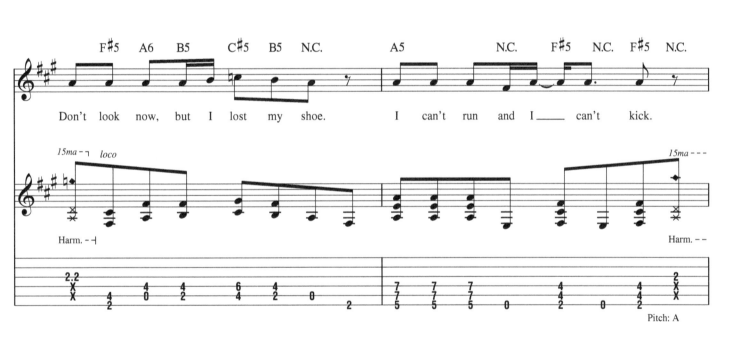

Don't look now, but I lost my shoe. I can't run and I _ can't kick.

What's a mat-ter, babe, are you feel-in' sick? What's a mat-ter, what's a mat-ter, what's a mat-ter you?

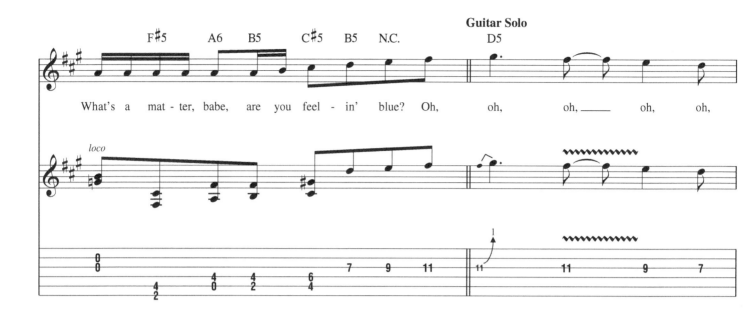

**Guitar Solo**

What's a mat - ter, babe, are you feel - in' blue? Oh, oh, oh, ___ oh, oh,

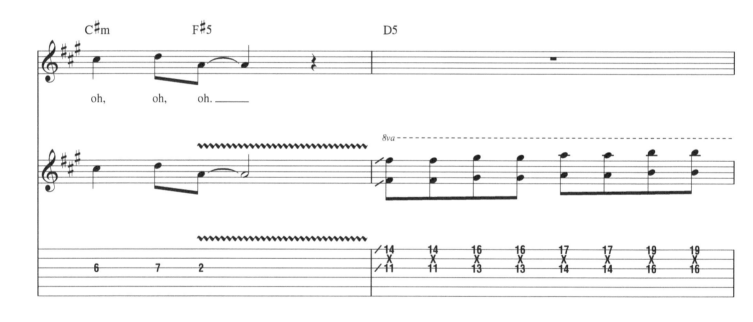

oh, oh, oh. ___

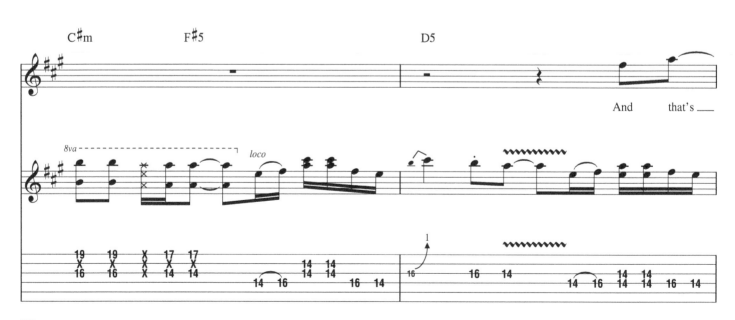

And that's ___

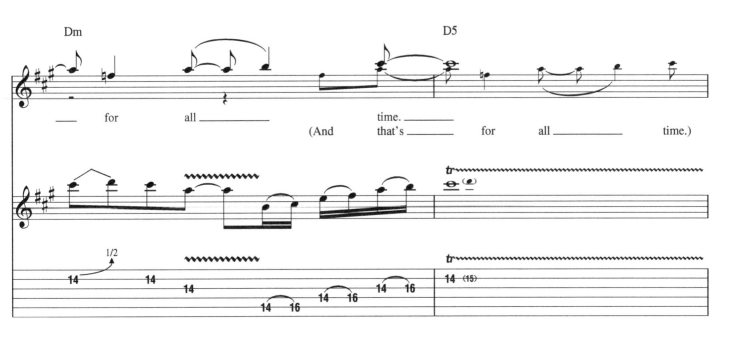

**D.S. al Coda 2**      ⊕ **Coda 2**

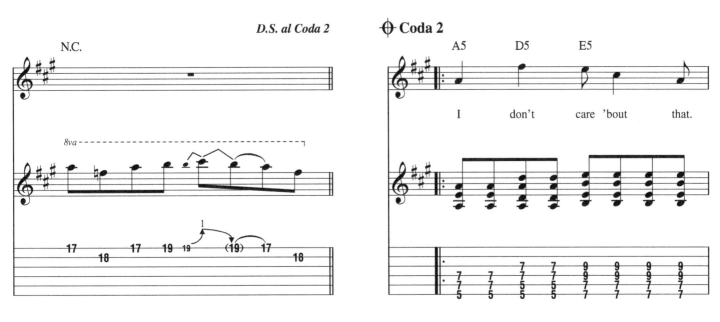

I   don't   care 'bout   that.

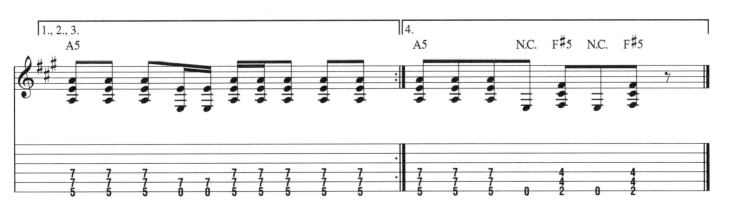

*Additional Lyrics*

2. Don't you ever fear, I'm always near.
   I know that you need help.
   Your tongue is twisted, your eyes are slit.
   You need a guardian.

# Dope Nose

### Words and Music by Rivers Cuomo

*Bass plays notes to right of slash throughout.

**Interlude**

Oh, _____ oh, _____ whoa, _____

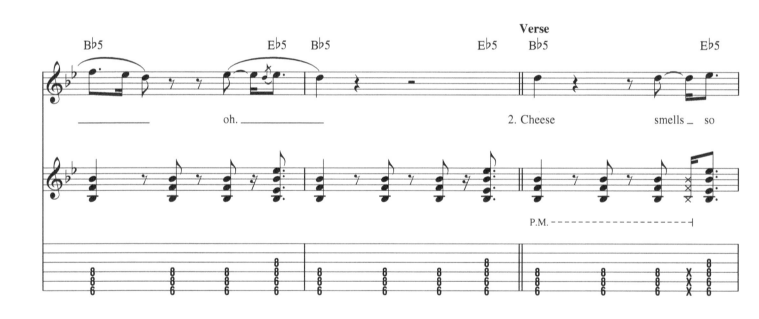

**Verse**

_____ oh. _____ 2. Cheese smells _ so

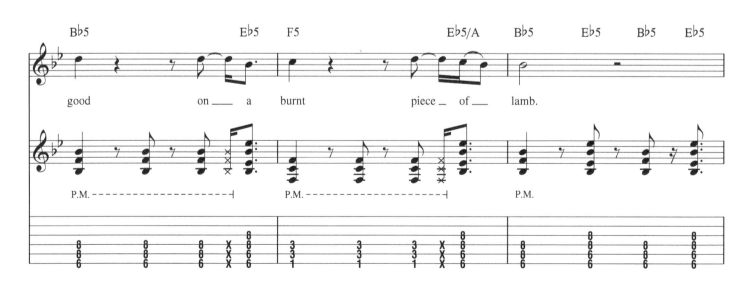

good on _ a burnt piece _ of _ lamb.

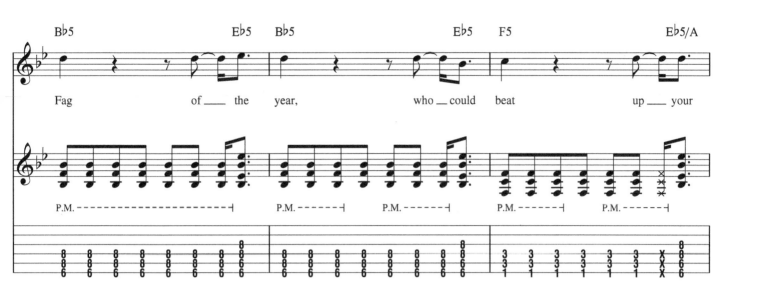

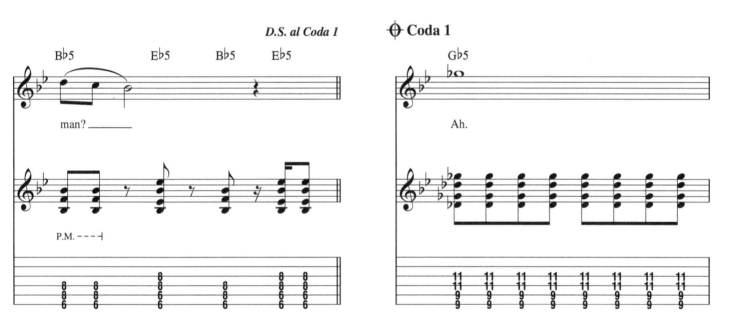

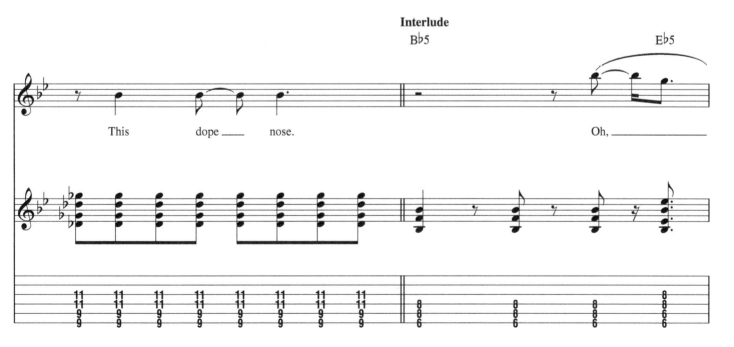

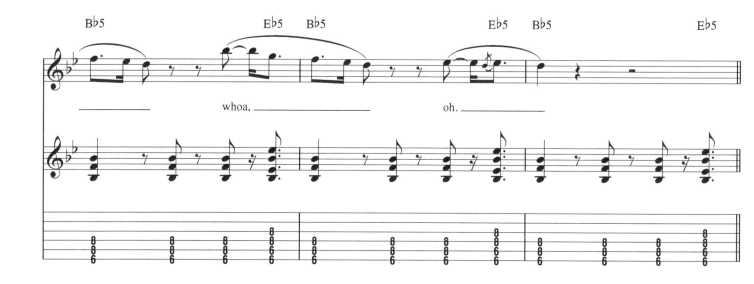

whoa, _____ oh. _____

**Guitar Solo**

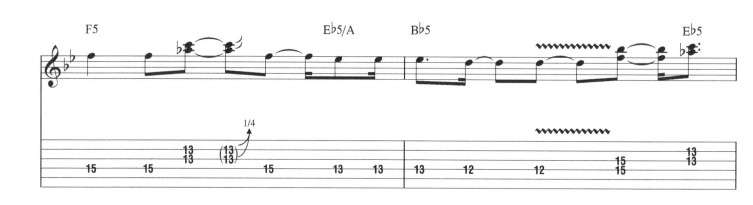

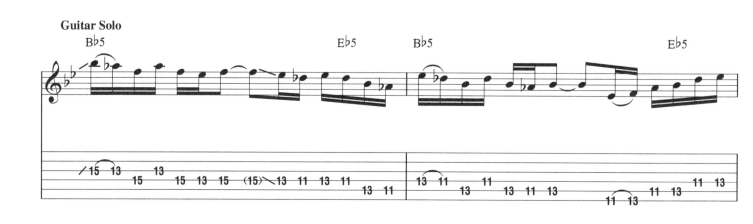

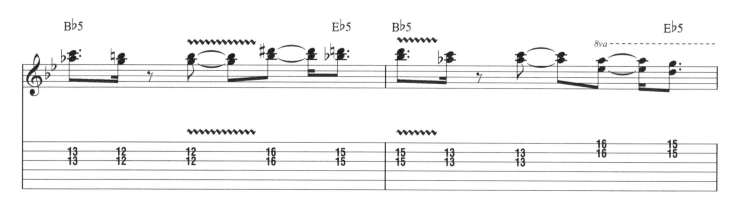

# My Name Is Jonas

### Words and Music by Rivers Cuomo, Jason Cropper and Patrick Wilson

Tune down 1/2 step:
(low to high) E♭-A♭-D♭-G♭-B♭-E♭

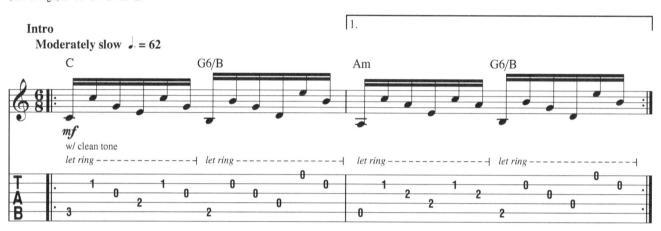

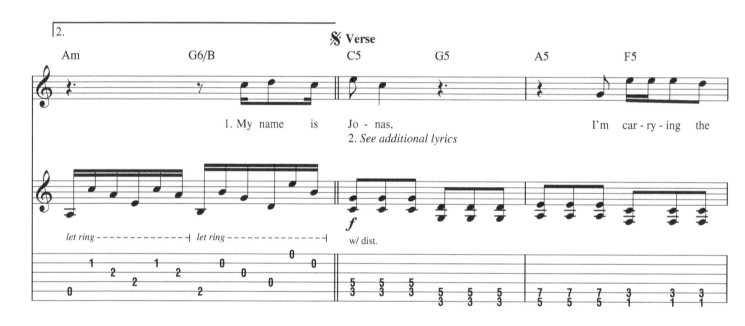

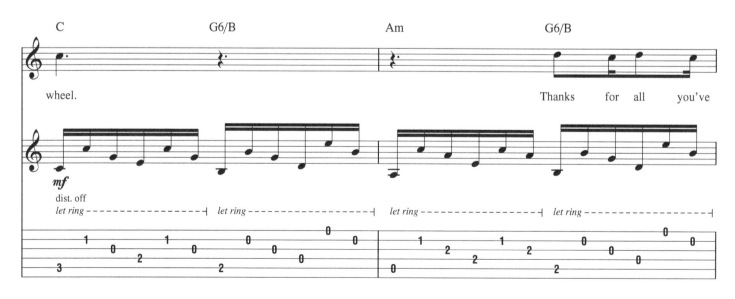

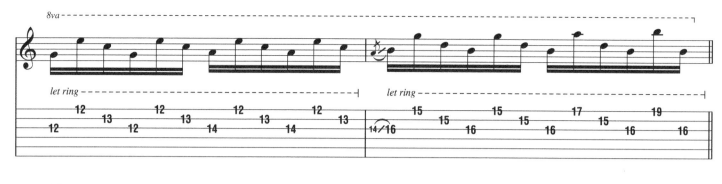

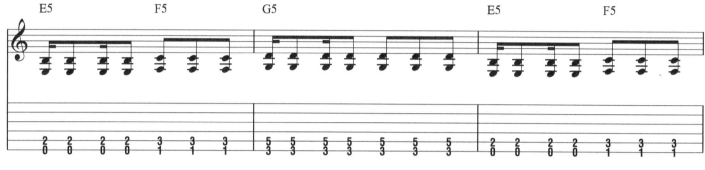

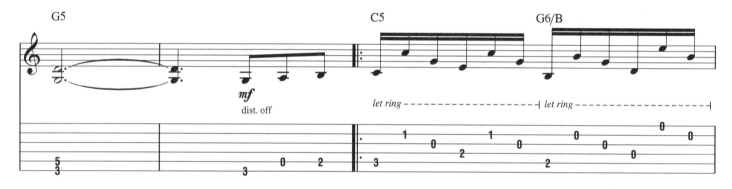

My name is Jo - nas.

*Additional Lyrics*

2. My name is Wepeel, got a box full of your toys.
   Fresh out of batteries, but they're still makin' noise, makin' noise.
   Tell me what to do, now the tank is dry.
   Now this wheel, it's flat, and you know what else?
   Guess what I received in the mail today.
   Words of deep concern from my little brother.
   The building's not goin' as he planned.
   The foreman has injured his hand.
   The dozer will not clear a path.
   The driver swears he learned his math.

# Say It Ain't So

## Words and Music by Rivers Cuomo

Tune down 1/2 step:
(low to high) E♭–A♭–D♭–G♭–B♭–E♭

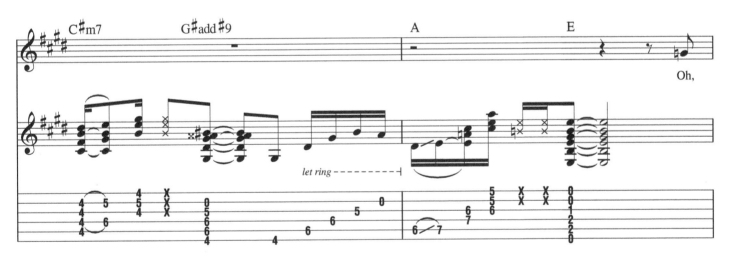

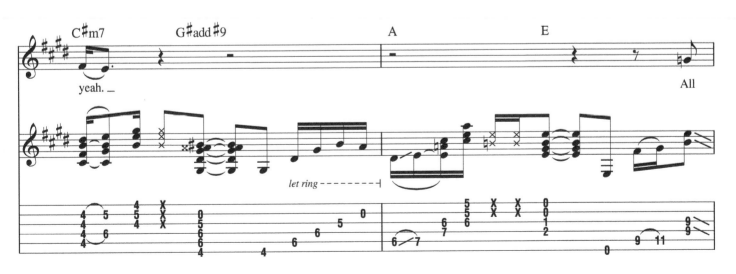

## Chorus
3rd time, substitute Fill 1

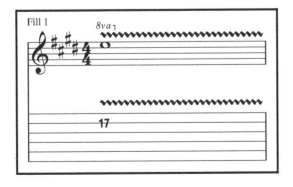

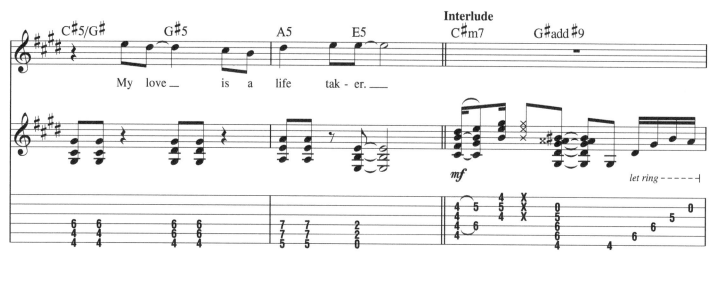

My love __ is a life tak - er. __

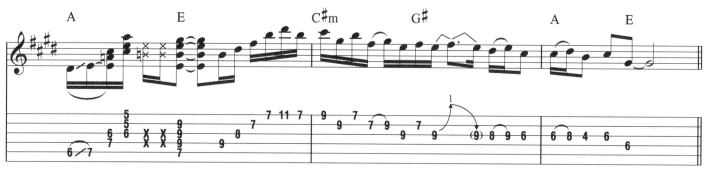

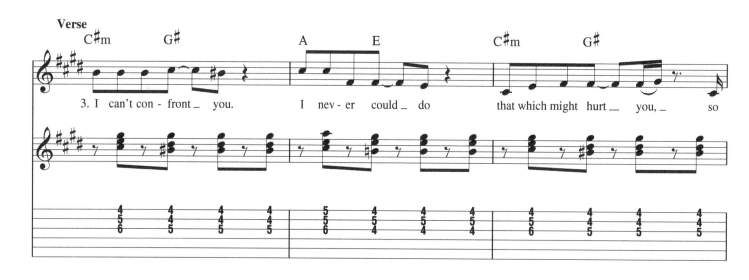

**Verse**

3. I can't con - front __ you.    I nev - er could __ do    that which might hurt __ you, __ so

try and be cool. _____    When I say    this way __    is a

*Additional Lyrics*

2. Flip on the tele', wrestle with Jimmy.
   Something is a bubbling behind my back.
   The bottle is ready to blow.

# Pork and Beans

Words and Music by Rivers Cuomo

Tune down 1/2 step:
(low to high) E♭-A♭-D♭-G♭-B♭-E♭

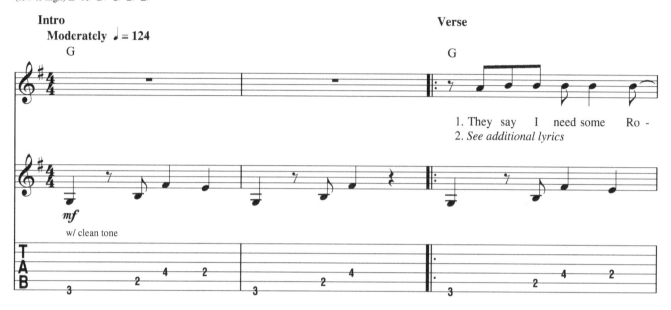

*Additional Lyrics*

2. Ev'ryone likes to dance to a happy song
   With a catchy chorus and beat so they can sing along.
   Timbaland knows the way to reach the top of the chart.
   Maybe if I work with him I can perfect the art.

# Undone – The Sweater Song

## Words and Music by Rivers Cuomo

Tune down 1/2 step:
(low to high) E♭-A♭-D♭-G♭-B♭-E♭

**Intro**
**Slow Rock** ♩ = 80

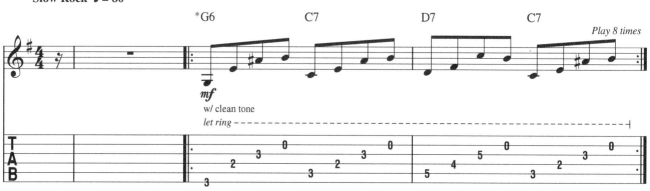

w/ clean tone
let ring ------------------------------------------------------------

*Chord symbols reflect basic harmony.

1. I'm me, __ me be, God damn, __ I am. I can __ sing and
2. *See additional lyrics*

hear me, __ know me. If you want to de - stroy my sweat-er, __

w/ dist.

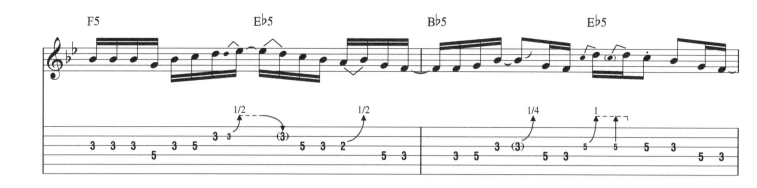

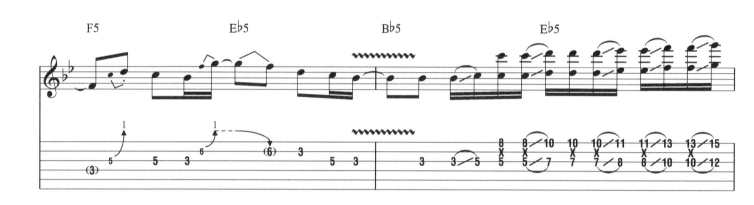

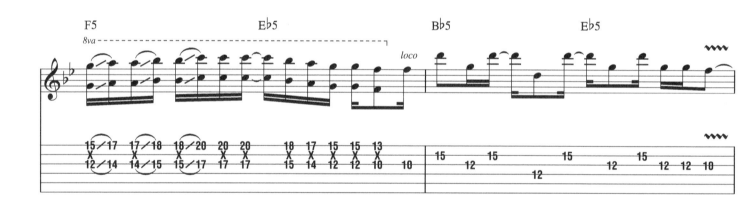

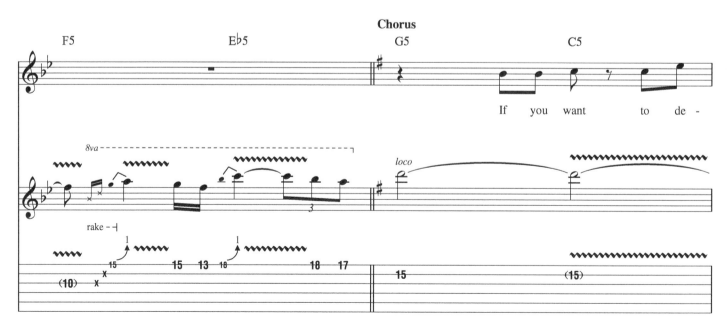

**Chorus**

If you want to de -

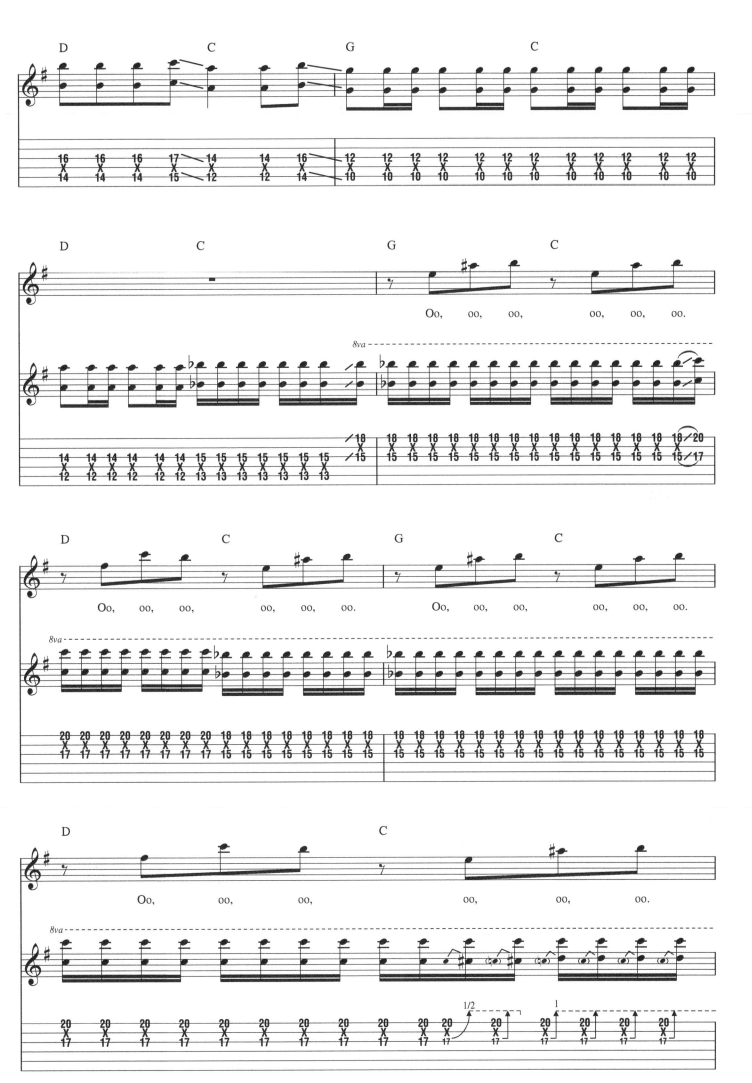

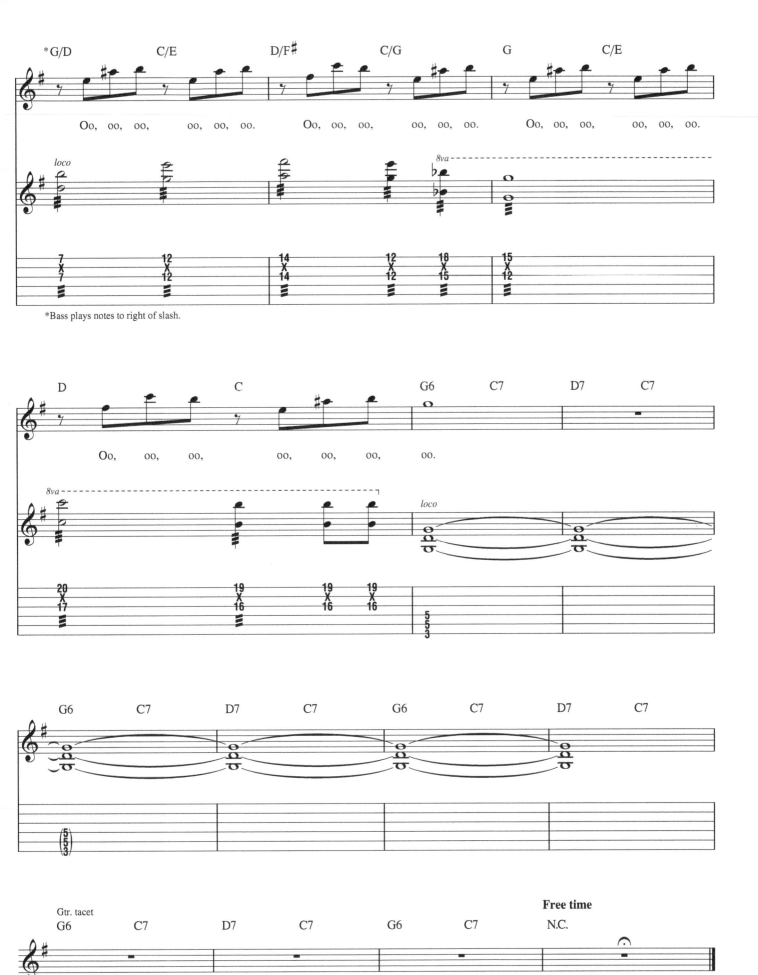

*Bass plays notes to right of slash.

Oo, oo, oo, oo, oo, oo. Oo, oo, oo, oo, oo, oo. Oo, oo, oo, oo, oo, oo.

Oo, oo, oo, oo, oo, oo, oo.

*Additional Lyrics*

2. Oh no, it go, it gone, bye bye.
   Who I, I think, I sink, and I die.

# HAL•LEONARD GUITAR PLAY-ALONG

INCLUDES TAB
AUDIO ACCESS INCLUDED

This series will help you play your favorite songs quickly and easily. Just follow the tab and listen to the audio to hear how the guitar should sound, and then play along using the separate backing tracks.

Playback tools are provided for slowing down the tempo without changing pitch and looping challenging parts. The melody and lyrics are included in the book so that you can sing or simply follow along.

**5. LATIN**
700939 .......................... $16.99

**6. WEEZER**
700958 .......................... $14.99

**7. CREAM**
701069 .......................... $16.99

**8. THE WHO**
701053 .......................... $16.99

**9. STEVE MILLER**
701054 .......................... $19.99

**0. SLIDE GUITAR HITS**
701055 .......................... $16.99

**1. JOHN MELLENCAMP**
701056 .......................... $14.99

**2. QUEEN**
701052 .......................... $16.99

**3. JIM CROCE**
701058 .......................... $17.99

**4. BON JOVI**
701060 .......................... $16.99

**5. JOHNNY CASH**
701070 .......................... $16.99

**6. THE VENTURES**
701124 .......................... $17.99

**7. BRAD PAISLEY**
701224 .......................... $16.99

**8. ERIC JOHNSON**
701353 .......................... $16.99

**9. AC/DC CLASSICS**
701356 .......................... $17.99

**20. PROGRESSIVE ROCK**
701457 .......................... $14.99

**21. U2**
701508 .......................... $16.99

**22. CROSBY, STILLS & NASH**
701610 .......................... $16.99

**23. LENNON & McCARTNEY ACOUSTIC**
701614 .......................... $16.99

**24. SMOOTH JAZZ**
200664 .......................... $16.99

**25. JEFF BECK**
701687 .......................... $17.99

**26. BOB MARLEY**
701701 .......................... $17.99

**27. 1970S ROCK**
701739 .......................... $16.99

**28. 1960S ROCK**
701740 .......................... $14.99

**129. MEGADETH**
00701741 .......................... $17.99

**130. IRON MAIDEN**
00701742 .......................... $17.99

**131. 1990S ROCK**
00701743 .......................... $14.99

**132. COUNTRY ROCK**
00701757 .......................... $15.99

**133. TAYLOR SWIFT**
00701894 .......................... $16.99

**134. AVENGED SEVENFOLD**
00701906 .......................... $16.99

**135. MINOR BLUES**
00151350 .......................... $17.99

**136. GUITAR THEMES**
00701922 .......................... $14.99

**137. IRISH TUNES**
00701966 .......................... $15.99

**138. BLUEGRASS CLASSICS**
00701967 .......................... $17.99

**139. GARY MOORE**
00702370 .......................... $16.99

**140. MORE STEVIE RAY VAUGHAN**
00702396 .......................... $17.99

**141. ACOUSTIC HITS**
00702401 .......................... $16.99

**142. GEORGE HARRISON**
00237697 .......................... $17.99

**143. SLASH**
00702425 .......................... $19.99

**144. DJANGO REINHARDT**
00702531 .......................... $16.99

**145. DEF LEPPARD**
00702532 .......................... $19.99

**146. ROBERT JOHNSON**
00702533 .......................... $16.99

**147. SIMON & GARFUNKEL**
14041591 .......................... $16.99

**148. BOB DYLAN**
14041592 .......................... $16.99

**149. AC/DC HITS**
14041593 .......................... $17.99

**150. ZAKK WYLDE**
02501717 .......................... $19.99

**151. J.S. BACH**
02501730 .......................... $16.99

**152. JOE BONAMASSA**
02501751 .......................... $19.99

**153. RED HOT CHILI PEPPERS**
00702990 .......................... $19.99

**155. ERIC CLAPTON – FROM THE ALBUM UNPLUGGED**
00703085 .......................... $16.99

**156. SLAYER**
00703770 .......................... $19.99

**157. FLEETWOOD MAC**
00101382 .......................... $17.99

**159. WES MONTGOMERY**
00102593 .......................... $19.99

**160. T-BONE WALKER**
00102641 .......................... $17.99

**161. THE EAGLES – ACOUSTIC**
00102659 .......................... $17.99

**162. THE EAGLES HITS**
00102667 .......................... $17.99

**163. PANTERA**
00103036 .......................... $17.99

**164. VAN HALEN 1986-1995**
00110270 .......................... $17.99

**165. GREEN DAY**
00210343 .......................... $17.99

**166. MODERN BLUES**
00700764 .......................... $16.99

**167. DREAM THEATER**
00111938 .......................... $24.99

**168. KISS**
00113421 .......................... $17.99

**169. TAYLOR SWIFT**
00115982 .......................... $16.99

**170. THREE DAYS GRACE**
00117337 .......................... $16.99

**171. JAMES BROWN**
00117420 .......................... $16.99

**172. THE DOOBIE BROTHERS**
00116970 .......................... $16.99

**173. TRANS-SIBERIAN ORCHESTRA**
00119907 .......................... $19.99

**174. SCORPIONS**
00122119 .......................... $16.99

**175. MICHAEL SCHENKER**
00122127 .......................... $17.99

**176. BLUES BREAKERS WITH JOHN MAYALL & ERIC CLAPTON**
00122132 .......................... $19.99

**177. ALBERT KING**
00123271 .......................... $16.99

**178. JASON MRAZ**
00124165 .......................... $17.99

**179. RAMONES**
00127073 .......................... $16.99

**180. BRUNO MARS**
00129706 .......................... $16.99

**181. JACK JOHNSON**
00129854 .......................... $16.99

**182. SOUNDGARDEN**
00138161 .......................... $17.99

**183. BUDDY GUY**
00138240 .......................... $17.99

**184. KENNY WAYNE SHEPHERD**
00138258 .......................... $17.99

**185. JOE SATRIANI**
00139457 .......................... $17.99

**186. GRATEFUL DEAD**
00139459 .......................... $17.99

**187. JOHN DENVER**
00140839 .......................... $17.99

**188. MÖTLEY CRÜE**
00141145 .......................... $17.99

**189. JOHN MAYER**
00144350 .......................... $17.99

**190. DEEP PURPLE**
00146152 .......................... $17.99

**191. PINK FLOYD CLASSICS**
00146164 .......................... $17.99

**192. JUDAS PRIEST**
00151352 .......................... $17.99

**193. STEVE VAI**
00156028 .......................... $19.99

**194. PEARL JAM**
00157925 .......................... $17.99

**195. METALLICA: 1983-1988**
00234291 .......................... $19.99

**196. METALLICA: 1991-2016**
00234292 .......................... $19.99

## HAL•LEONARD®

For complete songlists, visit
Hal Leonard online at
**www.halleonard.com**

Prices, contents, and availability subject to
change without notice.

# RECORDED VERSIONS®

## The Best Note-For-Note Transcriptions Available

**AUTHENTIC TRANSCRIPTIONS
WITH NOTES AND TABLATURE**

| | | |
|---|---|---|
| 00690603 | Aerosmith – O Yeah! Ultimate Hits ... | $29.99 |
| 00690178 | Alice in Chains – Acoustic | $22.99 |
| 00694865 | Alice in Chains – Dirt | $19.99 |
| 00694925 | Alice in Chains – Jar of Flies/Sap | $19.99 |
| 00691091 | Alice Cooper – Best of | $24.99 |
| 00690958 | Duane Allman – Guitar Anthology | $29.99 |
| 00694932 | Allman Brothers Band – Volume 1 | $29.99 |
| 00694933 | Allman Brothers Band – Volume 2 | $27.99 |
| 00694934 | Allman Brothers Band – Volume 3 | $29.99 |
| 00690945 | Alter Bridge – Blackbird | $24.99 |
| 00123558 | Arctic Monkeys – AM | $24.99 |
| 00214869 | Avenged Sevenfold – Best of 2005-2013 | $24.99 |
| 00690489 | Beatles – 1 | $24.99 |
| 00694929 | Beatles – 1962-1966 | $27.99 |
| 00694930 | Beatles – 1967-1970 | $29.99 |
| 00694880 | Beatles – Abbey Road | $19.99 |
| 00694832 | Beatles – Acoustic Guitar | $27.99 |
| 00690110 | Beatles – White Album (Book 1) | $19.99 |
| 00692385 | Chuck Berry | $24.99 |
| 00147787 | Black Crowes – Best of | $24.99 |
| 00690149 | Black Sabbath | $19.99 |
| 00690901 | Black Sabbath – Best of | $22.99 |
| 00691010 | Black Sabbath – Heaven and Hell | $22.99 |
| 00690148 | Black Sabbath – Master of Reality | $19.99 |
| 00690142 | Black Sabbath – Paranoid | $17.99 |
| 00148544 | Michael Bloomfield – Guitar Anthology | $24.99 |
| 00158600 | Joe Bonamassa – Blues of Desperation | $24.99 |
| 00198117 | Joe Bonamassa – Muddy Wolf at Red Rocks | $24.99 |
| 00283540 | Joe Bonamassa – Redemption | $24.99 |
| 00358863 | Joe Bonamassa – Royal Tea | $24.99 |
| 00690913 | Boston | $19.99 |
| 00690491 | David Bowie – Best of | $22.99 |
| 00286503 | Big Bill Broonzy – Guitar Collection | $19.99 |
| 00690261 | The Carter Family Collection | $19.99 |
| 00691079 | Johnny Cash – Best of | $24.99 |
| 00690936 | Eric Clapton – Complete Clapton | $34.99 |
| 00694869 | Eric Clapton – Unplugged | $24.99 |
| 00124873 | Eric Clapton – Unplugged (Deluxe) | $29.99 |
| 00138731 | Eric Clapton & Friends – The Breeze | $24.99 |
| 00139967 | Coheed & Cambria – In Keeping Secrets of Silent Earth: 3 | $24.99 |
| 00141704 | Jesse Cook – Works, Vol. 1 | $19.99 |
| 00288787 | Creed – Greatest Hits | $22.99 |
| 00690819 | Creedence Clearwater Revival | $27.99 |
| 00690648 | Jim Croce – Very Best of | $19.99 |
| 00690572 | Steve Cropper – Soul Man | $22.99 |
| 00690613 | Crosby, Stills & Nash – Best of | $29.99 |
| 00690784 | Def Leppard – Best of | $24.99 |
| 00694831 | Derek and the Dominos – Layla & Other Assorted Love Songs | $24.99 |
| 00291164 | Dream Theater – Distance Over Time | $24.99 |
| 00278631 | Eagles – Greatest Hits 1971-1975 | $22.99 |
| 00278632 | Eagles – Very Best of | $39.99 |
| 00690515 | Extreme II – Pornograffiti | $24.99 |
| 00150257 | John Fahey – Guitar Anthology | $24.99 |
| 00690664 | Fleetwood Mac – Best of | $24.99 |
| 00691024 | Foo Fighters – Greatest Hits | $24.99 |
| 00120220 | Robben Ford – Guitar Anthology | $29.99 |
| 00295410 | Rory Gallagher – Blues | $24.99 |
| 00139460 | Grateful Dead – Guitar Anthology | $29.99 |
| 00691190 | Peter Green – Best of | $24.99 |

| | | |
|---|---|---|
| 00287517 | Greta Van Fleet – Anthem of the Peaceful Army | $19.99 |
| 00287515 | Greta Van Fleet – From the Fires | $19.99 |
| 00694798 | George Harrison – Anthology | $24.99 |
| 00692930 | Jimi Hendrix – Are You Experienced? | $29.99 |
| 00692931 | Jimi Hendrix – Axis: Bold As Love | $24.99 |
| 00690304 | Jimi Hendrix – Band of Gypsys | $24.99 |
| 00694944 | Jimi Hendrix – Blues | $29.99 |
| 00692932 | Jimi Hendrix – Electric Ladyland | $27.99 |
| 00660029 | Buddy Holly – Best of | $24.99 |
| 00200446 | Iron Maiden – Guitar Tab | $29.99 |
| 00694912 | Eric Johnson – Ah Via Musicom | $24.99 |
| 00690271 | Robert Johnson – Transcriptions | $27.99 |
| 00690427 | Judas Priest – Best of | $24.99 |
| 00690492 | B.B. King – Anthology | $29.99 |
| 00130447 | B.B. King – Live at the Regal | $19.99 |
| 00690134 | Freddie King – Collection | $22.99 |
| 00327968 | Marcus King – El Dorado | $22.99 |
| 00690157 | Kiss – Alive | $19.99 |
| 00690356 | Kiss – Alive II | $24.99 |
| 00291163 | Kiss – Very Best of | $24.99 |
| 00345767 | Greg Koch – Best of | $29.99 |
| 00690377 | Kris Kristofferson – Guitar Collection | $22.99 |
| 00690834 | Lamb of God – Ashes of the Wake | $24.99 |
| 00690525 | George Lynch – Best of | $29.99 |
| 00690955 | Lynyrd Skynyrd – All-Time Greatest Hits | $24.99 |
| 00694954 | Lynyrd Skynyrd – New Best of | $24.99 |
| 00690577 | Yngwie Malmsteen – Anthology | $29.99 |
| 00694896 | John Mayall with Eric Clapton – Blues Breakers | $19.99 |
| 00694952 | Megadeth – Countdown to Extinction | $24.99 |
| 00276065 | Megadeth – Greatest Hits: Back to the Start | $24.99 |
| 00694951 | Megadeth – Rust in Peace | $27.99 |
| 00690011 | Megadeth – Youthanasia | $24.99 |
| 00209876 | Metallica – Hardwired to Self-Destruct | $24.99 |
| 00690646 | Pat Metheny – One Quiet Night | $24.99 |
| 00102591 | Wes Montgomery – Guitar Anthology | $27.99 |
| 00691092 | Gary Moore – Best of | $27.99 |
| 00694802 | Gary Moore – Still Got the Blues | $24.99 |
| 00355456 | Alanis Morisette – Jagged Little Pill | $22.99 |
| 00690611 | Nirvana | $24.99 |
| 00694913 | Nirvana – In Utero | $22.99 |
| 00694883 | Nirvana – Nevermind | $19.99 |
| 00690026 | Nirvana – Unplugged in New York | $19.99 |
| 00265439 | Nothing More – Tab Collection | $24.99 |
| 00243349 | Opeth – Best of | $22.99 |
| 00690499 | Tom Petty – Definitive Guitar Collection | $29.99 |
| 00121933 | Pink Floyd – Acoustic Guitar Collection | $27.99 |
| 00690428 | Pink Floyd – Dark Side of the Moon | $22.99 |
| 00244637 | Pink Floyd – Guitar Anthology | $24.99 |
| 00239799 | Pink Floyd – The Wall | $24.99 |
| 00690789 | Poison – Best of | $22.99 |
| 00690925 | Prince – Very Best of | $24.99 |
| 00690003 | Queen – Classic Queen | $24.99 |
| 00694975 | Queen – Greatest Hits | $25.99 |
| 00694910 | Rage Against the Machine | $22.99 |
| 00119834 | Rage Against the Machine – Guitar Anthology | $24.99 |
| 00690426 | Ratt – Best of | $24.99 |
| 00690055 | Red Hot Chili Peppers – Blood Sugar Sex Magik | $19.99 |

| | | |
|---|---|---|
| 00690379 | Red Hot Chili Peppers – Californication | $22.9 |
| 00690673 | Red Hot Chili Peppers – Greatest Hits | $22.9 |
| 00690852 | Red Hot Chili Peppers – Stadium Arcadium | $29.9 |
| 00690511 | Django Reinhardt – Definitive Collection | $24.9 |
| 00690014 | Rolling Stones – Exile on Main Street | $24.9 |
| 00690631 | Rolling Stones – Guitar Anthology | $34.9 |
| 00323854 | Rush – The Spirit of Radio: Greatest Hits, 1974-1987 | $22.9 |
| 00173534 | Santana – Guitar Anthology | $29.9 |
| 00276350 | Joe Satriani – What Happens Next | $24.9 |
| 00690566 | Scorpions – Best of | $24.9 |
| 00690604 | Bob Seger – Guitar Collection | $24.9 |
| 00234543 | Ed Sheeran – Divide* | $19.9 |
| 00691114 | Slash – Guitar Anthology | $34.9 |
| 00690813 | Slayer – Guitar Collection | $24.9 |
| 00690419 | Slipknot | $19.9 |
| 00316982 | Smashing Pumpkins – Greatest Hits | $22.9 |
| 00690912 | Soundgarden – Guitar Anthology | $24.9 |
| 00120004 | Steely Dan – Best of | $27.9 |
| 00322564 | Stone Temple Pilots – Thank You | $22.9 |
| 00690520 | Styx – Guitar Collection | $22.9 |
| 00120081 | Sublime | $19.9 |
| 00690531 | System of a Down – Toxicity | $19.9 |
| 00694824 | James Taylor – Best of | $19.9 |
| 00694887 | Thin Lizzy – Best of | $22.9 |
| 00253237 | Trivium – Guitar Tab Anthology | $24.9 |
| 00690683 | Robin Trower – Bridge of Sighs | $19.9 |
| 00156024 | Steve Vai – Guitar Anthology | $34.9 |
| 00660137 | Steve Vai – Passion & Warfare | $29.9 |
| 00295076 | Van Halen – 30 Classics | $29.9 |
| 00690024 | Stevie Ray Vaughan – Couldn't Stand the Weather | $19.9 |
| 00660058 | Stevie Ray Vaughan – Lightnin' Blues 1983-1987 | $29.9 |
| 00217455 | Stevie Ray Vaughan – Plays Slow Blues | $24.9 |
| 00694835 | Stevie Ray Vaughan – The Sky Is Crying | $24.9 |
| 00690015 | Stevie Ray Vaughan – Texas Flood | $22.9 |
| 00694789 | Muddy Waters – Deep Blues | $27.9 |
| 00152161 | Doc Watson – Guitar Anthology | $24.9 |
| 00690071 | Weezer (The Blue Album) | $22.9 |
| 00237811 | White Stripes – Greatest Hits | $24.9 |
| 00117511 | Whitesnake – Guitar Collection | $24.9 |
| 00122303 | Yes – Guitar Collection | $24.9 |
| 00690443 | Frank Zappa – Hot Rats | $22.9 |
| 00121684 | ZZ Top – Early Classics | $27.9 |
| 00690589 | ZZ Top – Guitar Anthology | $24.9 |

**COMPLETE SERIES LIST ONLINE!**

## HAL•LEONARD
www.halleonard.com

Prices and availability subject to change without notice.
*Tab transcriptions only.

012
27